ACCIDENTAL
OCCIDENTAL

To Ma,

A fellow Bohemian poet.

with warmest wishes

Dave MᶜLindy

23 - 5 - 11

A Chameleon Press book

ACCIDENTAL OCCIDENTAL
ISBN 978-988-99565-9-2

© 2005, 2010 David McKirdy

Published by Chameleon Press Ltd.
22/F, 253-261 Hennessy Road, Wanchai, Hong Kong
www.chameleonpress.com

Printed in Hong Kong
First printing this edition 2011

The original hardcover edition of this book (2005) was supported by

The Hong Kong Arts Development Council fully supports freedom of artistic expression.
The views and opinions expressed in this publication, and the entire contents thereof,
are those of the author and do not represent the stand of the Council.

ACCIDENTAL OCCIDENTAL

David McKirdy

chameleon press
hong kong

To my mum and dad

For the priceless gifts of love and possibilities

Preface to the new edition

The East-meets-West theme has probably been a well-worn cliché since before Genghis Khan set out to pursue his own unique brand of cultural dissemination, or perhaps that particular example could best be described as "insemination". My own perspective is somewhat more liberal and hopefully will result in a less traumatic experience for my interlocutors than an encounter with the great Khan.

I come to poetry quite late in life after completing a degree course in Humanities as a mature student at The Hong Kong Open University. Having been raised and educated in Hong Kong, I have always felt myself to be in the unique position of someone who definitely belongs in the city, but as a non-native, I still retain something of an outsider's perspective.

This, my first collection, fulfills two functions, that of seeking to find a distinctive poetic voice as well as selecting topics and themes on which I feel I can contribute some kind of valid comment. The subject matter contained within covers a range of subjects from the intensely personal, to political and social commentary and even my response to international news reports.

Hong Kong being a small place, poetry is as much a social activity as a written one. The writing of these poems coincided with numerous developments in Hong Kong's literary life, or at least the International and English-language aspects of it, from the founding of local English-language poetry circles (known as Outloud), to the setting up of The Hong Kong International Literary Festival, activities in which I played an active and pivotal role.

I feel that mine is as much an Asian voice as any of my Chinese contemporaries and a second collection, more focused on Asia in general and Hong Kong in particular, is on its way. Hopefully, my location in a Hakka fishing-village a stone's throw from the South China Sea will imbue these poems with some degree of authenticity; I hope at least some of them speak to you.

David McKirdy, Hong Kong, February 2011

Contents

Abroad in England

Descend the steps and taste the air
home from exile
arrived at last in Blake's green and pleasant land.
Through Sloane Square, Westminster, Marble Arch and Holborn.
Conveyed underground through history
in the quiet company of undistinguished fellow travellers.
Rich man, poor man, beggar man, thief
journey in insular isolation.
The only sounds the attack of wheels on rails
and the self conscious turning to page three.

Where's the spirit that held the world at its feet?
It kicks a ball now
colonized by mediocrity, xenophobia, tattooed housewives,
and the deification of the lout and the under-achiever.

But still a nation of shopkeepers,
Asians mainly,
vending micro-wave meals, football, tits and beer,
the latest opiates for the masses.
A weekly bath, but soap every night on TV depicts
lives more mundane than their own,
played by graduates from RADA with cockney elocution.
"Alas poor Yorick, wot a prat."
Dross dressed as entertainment, masquerading as art.
Exciting inanity, mundane urbanity.

No sign of Jeeves and Wooster, or genteel decay,
or cricket on village greens,
or scholarly gents in trilby hats,
or courtesy, efficiency, or care.

I came to find my centre and see my place of birth
an ideological -We won the bloody war- Englishman
visiting a post-war, post-empire, post-punk outpost
to confirm some utopian vision and the lies propagated in school.
A madness fostered by too much distance and too much time
masked my total alienation from this totally alien nation.
So I'll return cynically, clinically wiser,
an accidental occidental, re-oriented
to where my homely heart is
East of Suez. Far East and away.

Inspiration

A writer
needs to feel stress, strain, angst,
needs to experience bad times, sad times, hard times,
needs to bleed, sweat and cry,
in order to write from life.
Real life.

My parents never hit or abused me.
They supported my dreams and aspirations,
spent time as a family and never divorced,
refrained from eating any of the children when times were tough,
provided a good education,
instilled a social conscience in me,
and loved with equality.
They were saints.

The bastards!

Self portrait

I've got a picture in my mind,
a self-portrait of me at nineteen.
I've felt nineteen,
I've been nineteen for twenty-five years.
A Dorian Gray in reverse.
My body ages but the mental self-image remains
a psychological construct
untouched by arthritis, grey hairs and haemorrhoids.

Will I ever see the face in the mirror
instead of the one in the attic
and will the knife finally slice that imaginary canvas,
cut the cord of my illusions?

Kids grow up too fast these days.
overnight is all very well
but a quarter of a century in one day.
Not me! I'm staying young in spirit,
young at heart for as long as I can.
I'll show you mine if you show me yours.

Cod philosophy

"Pass the pepper if you please."
"Nice weather for time of year."
Idle pleasant chatter
a conversational hors-d'oeuvre
preceding watery platitudes
and stodgy indigestible opinions.
I hold my smile on a stick
like a carnival mask
and mentally mark the minutes
like a cheap watch
strapped to your wrist.
How resourceful
to recycle old new-views
gleaned from the wrapper of your last fish supper.
Potted, editorialized and claimed as your own
authoritative discourse on tabloid topics.
How skillfully you wield
eight column inches in your hand.

Wanker!

My old man

Old man of the street,
outside, on the margins.
Another waste product of our society
no longer in it, but undeniably of it.
You exist amidst parked cars
with your bric-a-brac fortune; discarded shards of other's lives.
Your whole world lies in two cardboard cartons and a plastic pail,
piled high and pushed on a broken-wheeled barrow.

You spend your days sleeping, watching
and smoking dog-eared dog-ends.
Never begging
but accepting any largesse that comes your way.
I never see anyone talk to you, converse with you.
Except for me, but I talk to babies, dogs and trees!
"Uncle, have you eaten yet?"
"Here's a twenty for morning tea."

You're old enough to be my father,
old enough to be many fathers.
What wisdom lies lost
beyond those sparkling eyes
and lopsided toothless smile?
You epitomise the ultimate endgame of life.
Showing kindness to you
is showing kindness to our future selves.

Photograph, Amber Matthews

Pole dancer

Pole dancer: Taxi-girl
A ripe cherry plucked from poverty
Another executive stress toy
to market in a brave new world.

End user: Sad bastard
Cirrhotic lone drinker
on the home stretch to a place
only there in his mind.
Self-deluding flattery
static flaccid body and a wandering bloodshot eye.

What can he think she sees in him
as she homes in with her smile
and soporific sweet nothings?
The wife no longer wants to understand
but this girl deeply comprehends
everything she needs to know.
Sfumato-smile, predatory Gioconda. Anaconda!
A latter-day Salome
her John's head on a platter
her hand in his pocket.

Squalid symbiotic sadness
Together they dance alone.

Curtain call

Is it that time already?
I'm caught unprepared
I thought there was time left to spare.
But as your light dims and sputters
you pass me the torch
a weight too heavy to bear.
And now, stripped of all illusion of control, I teeter
unbalanced on the edge of something bigger.
Then, drawn moth-like, fleeing falling
flying naked towards the flame.

With your hand on my shoulder
that unbearable burden suddenly incandescent,
lighter than air.
You carry me still
as you carried me then
younger than I am now.
I see my future reflected in you
as you see yours in me.
You move aside, I take your place
no longer your understudy.

We'll act out this last scene together as one
and may yet steal the show or a smile.

A game of marbles

I sit among the Grecian ruins
and contemplate for half a day
prototype pillars of Western pride.
Marble and ideas
stolen from the ancient world.
Euclidean proportions, Democratic ideals.
Stolen, but proffered free for all
as a condition of foreign aid.
to third class, third world citizens
needing daily bread
working like Trojans.

Hospitality

My friend Jo and I both went to hospital today.
If only we had gone together
we could have taken the place apart.
She who, with a single slap,
once knocked a man to the ground,
after he had touched her breast.
And me who could bullshit for Britain.
Unfortunately we went to different hospitals
and ended up alone and vulnerable,
sick and at the mercy of people who don't give a shit.
Different hospitals, same story!
In places dedicated to the care of people
why does nobody care?

The tree of life

It seemed like forty days and nights the rains came down
wiping away all that was bad and good
both trespasser and trespassed against
swallowed by torrents of life-giving, life-taking water.
In mother Africa the cradle of humanity
the second coming was long foretold.
the Christ child 'El Nino'.
Dramatic, climatic, climactic change.
Global warming, a gift from the developed world
and for the sins of those fathers others endure a ritual cleansing
Death and Rebirth.

After the deluge new life stirs
across an immeasurable expanse of water
punctuated only by the upstretched limbs of supplicant trees.
Man and machine fly to and fro
weapons of war entrusted with a holier mission.
To rescue the one heavy with child
labouring in those cradling boughs.
That blessed infant delivered from evil by a strangers hand
tethered to a shimmering silver umbilical of hope.
Ascending towards the warming sun
as the haloed warbirds wings whirl and churn the air.
Redemption at the very moment of birth
a Lazarus child of the new millennium
a link between the water and the land
a Piscean from Poseidon's holy realm.
Into our hands He commended this spirit
are we worthy of the task?

During March 2000 there was extensive flooding in Mozambique: there was a photograph in the paper of a woman giving birth in a tree assisted by the helicopter rescue services. The mother and a healthy baby were then winched to safety.

Hubris

I've been watching a friend descend
deeper and deeper into a black hole
from which I fear he may never return.
A consummate artist with intelligence
and talent and love in abundance
but something's gone wrong
everything's wrong!
Delusions of control, balance and normality
fueled by drink, drugs and insecurity.
There's a dark brooding shadow watching, waiting on walls.
Which way will he jump?
I've tried to coax him back from the edge
with offers of asylum and truth;
those telling titbits that don't taste too sweet.
I've been told to "fuck off!"

That's OK.
I'm not in such great shape myself
and I'm only offering love and a quiet room in paradise.
Maybe this is a test for both of us.
Can I offer help and then let go?
And then acknowledge
my own delusions of control?

Love works

Love works so well at a distance
a romantic spiritual arms length embrace.
Perfection guaranteed in the absence
of any body of evidence to the contrary.
The perfect union, a honeymoon twice a year
two weeks, just long enough
for friction-induced physical maladies
but not long enough for friction in social intercourse.

Then parting once again
with continued lovelorn platitudes
declaimed during endless melancholic phone calls
and condensed into florid flawed lyrical epistles.
Imaginative reruns of ecstatic joy
growing with distance and time:

The nape of the neck downy soft
the pleasing contour of a recumbent thigh
and the odorous musky afterglow of sweat and sweet declarations.
Intimate details of a puzzle ever evolving never resolved.

Idyllic scenarios exist so perfectly as day dreams,
which ease the denial of two separate lives

lived apart.

Sepia

I found a photo of my sister as a girl of sixteen,
not long before she embarked on her own shot at life.
By nineteen she was a wife and mother
living in a foreign land.

I missed her solicitous presence
but her departure left me an only son.
The baby, to be spoiled and indulged
and to benefit from battles
already fought by elder brother, elder sister
and won by default, a constant wearing down
and redrawing of lines in the sand;
Long hair - "No problem."
Ridiculous trousers - "He'll grow out of those eventually."
Red high heeled platform boots - "Hello Santa Claus!"
"Wear what you like, do what you like but DON'T TAKE DRUGS!"
Well they were tried and discarded along with golf and the violin.
Our parents try to mould and guide and turn us into something good
but they're wasting their time, love is enough.
When the cocoon opens
we flex our wings and fly away
and become what we become.

My sister is gone but forever alive
conserved within the amber of our hearts and living memory
and I still see my father daily, as a younger man
staring back at me through the mirror of time.

Expectations

Shuk Wah is a simple soul
found wanting in wit and wherewithal.
A little girl lost at twenty-six
a graceful flower fatally flawed.
But blessed with love in abundance;
the love of music
the love of life and
the love of anybody who meets her.
The worries of the world wash over her
softly flowing, touching briefly in passing
like a wise and well-worn river stone
and she in turn touches us.
Naive, unworldly, noble and trusting
she challenges us to meet no expectations but our own
reflected in the mirror of her soul.

Epistle to my unborn child

You missed your chance at life
because I jealously nurtured mine.
Because of commitment;
Absolute when it came to personal goals
absolutely lacking when it came to relationships
and letting go of fear and the baggage of insecurity.

I never gave myself permission to love or be loved.
The possibility of you frightened me in early years.
You were absent as a concept as I pursued fame and fortune
and the motorcycle world championship.
You merited not a thought as I traversed the world
entranced by the glamour of Formula One.

I matured reluctantly into a middle-aged teenager
and sought acclaim as a rock musician.
Your voice was seldom heard
just an occasional appearance in thoughts and dreams
and the nagging doubt
that time was passing by.

But now, as I more often put my thoughts on paper
you appear daily and appeal to me.
So many of my friends are fathers, mothers, grandfathers!
I'm twice a Godfather, but never the real thing.
Did I miss a chance, or did they?
Or have we missed it yet?

Missionary position

I was met by two guys in the street
with perfect, bright white teeth.
They wore bright white shirts
and neckties, in spite of the heat.
'Elder Smith' and 'Elder Young'
declared the black plastic tags on their breasts.
I was the elder of both added together.
So young and so sure of their mission
travelling in pairs to ward off Satan
and the temptation of a cup of tea.
They asked if I had heard the one true word.
I've heard many a true word, some spoken in jest!
They're collecting souls. So where do I sign?
And when can I collect my wives and my new teeth?

Their God was a white American in a white shirt.
They were right and everybody else was wrong.
At the end of their mission they'll be taking their souls
and going back home, to help make America great again.

Now that put the fear of God in me.

History lesson

A historian skillfully used documents and sources
to successfully prove—on paper— that the holocaust never occurred.
He was right it never occurred—on paper.
There was no paper in Auschwitz, Birkenau, Dachau, Sobibor...
just mountains of spectacles, shoes, gold teeth and nameless but
    numbered corpses.
Holders of one way tickets to oblivion or—even worse—survival.

But still, let's not get hung up on details.
The academic persevered and proved that:
Nice Mr. Hitler was kind to old ladies and animals.
A benevolent patriot who marched purely for health and
    recreation—
Into Poland, Czechoslovakia, Belgium, Holland, France...
Undoubtedly a keen traveler, an accidental tourist perhaps.
Some tourist.
Some accident.

Although he could prove it the historian made a mistake
the plausibility of his proof was dented in the face of living proof
in the face of common sense, in the face of common knowledge
and in the faces of those—still amongst us—
who had lived it and died it, not merely read it.
The tattooed and broken who somehow survived
the liberators who saw and were sick
and the guilty who escaped, or stayed—not bothering to run—citing
    lack of evidence.

So go to Dachau and try to deny your visceral reaction.
Your very bones will weep with the stained sterile earth.
Wooden guard towers reach into a sky
bleak beyond belief above barbed wire fences.
Stand there with closed, red-rimmed eyes and catarrhal voice and
    say;
"It never happened." TRY.

The saying goes:
"If history teaches us anything it's that we learn nothing from
    history."
Maybe it's just as well
when those who write history learn nothing from life.

April 2000, a British academic, David Irving, sued an American author, Deborah Lipstadt, for libel for describing him in a book as a holocaust-denier, anti-Semitic and a bigot. He lost the case.

Old friends

As I recall we used to be inseparable, or is my mind playing tricks
with the fondness of pondered reminiscences?
But by the time we met again, much anticipated with heightened
    senses
we were both somebody else.
Geometric divergent lines so far from our common starting point
the gap ever widening.

Astringent anticipation inflamed the wound
inflicted not by cruel words or actions
but by the lack of empathy.
A lack of any coincidence of achievements or dreams or goals
and the knowledge that we had both tried so hard.
Initial heightened expectations and enthusiasm
dwindling to a choked chuckle for retold boyhood adventures
of mountains scaled and battles won.
Naive childish reality, the sweet half-truths of youth
that make childhood a distant, hazy, utopian dream.

Reunions are dangerous things,
they make you analyse the present, and reassess the past.
They can disrupt your carefully constructed paradigm
and paralyse the paradise you hold so dear.
What really happened to you and me since we parted?
The bits between the lines, those details that make a life
not the high and low points that punctuate it.

There's you with your 2.4 kids and a Volvo
me with my set of drums.
Your mortgage and second car, second wife, second hand
me with my set of dreams
rumpled and creased, but still serviceable.
You exude a different humour now
a bleakness of spirit nips at your heels.
You made the grade, you made your bed
now you sleepwalk through life with credit-card credibility.
After final handshakes, declarations of desire for future contact
and a forced hypocritical embrace
we walk away, not looking back
each shrugging off the other's lingering aura and binning the name
    card.

No. Not again.
My own disappointments serve me well enough.

Bright future

'LITTLE BOY PLUCKED FROM THE SEA.' six years old.
A Cuban exile, now motherless child
shipwrecked and orphaned trying for liberty.
A pre-pubescent Robinson Crusoe
a minor cause célèbre.
Denied to his father and motherland
induced to stay with bribes of apple pie
Coke and Disneyworld.
Illegal Elian
a point scoring pawn in the game
between God-fearing Christians
and the Cuban in-Fidel.
"Keep the boy here," say the pundits, "there's a better life,
a brighter future for a six year old."

'LITTLE BOY SHOOTS LITTLE GIRL.' six years old.
Six years old no more.
A profligate waste of youth, life and human potential
both children lost in that cruel flash of fire.
Every mother cries for fear and sympathy
and the loss of innocence too young.
Presidents also cry - for votes - and vow to legislate.
"But it's already illegal!" say the lobbyists
"The lad possessed no permit to bear arms."
But he was permitted to live in a crack den with the big bad wolf
who huffed and puffed and blew his house down.
No fairy tale endings for this little boy
he's seen Goldilocks do smack with the three little pigs
and Snow White turn tricks for a line.
The sad reality of life on the jagged edge.
"If only!"
If only what?
He floundered so long in a sea of utter confusion
only plucked from danger too late, then put into care,
a quality absent so far in this land of plenty.
In God's own country
how many like him fall through the cracks?
Clocks.
Ticking... Ticking...

25 Nov. 1999. 6 year old Cuban Elian Gonzales, the only survivor from a shipwreck, was rescued by the Miami coast guard and became the subject of a protracted ideological and legal battle. Meanwhile on 29 Feb. 2000 a 6 year old American boy from a deprived background shot and killed one of his classmates, a 6 year old girl.

One heart

Italian surgeons tried to separate
two Peruvian babies with Siamese Karma
joined at the chest, sharing one heart.
A physical manifestation
of our most fervent sacred desire;
that oneness that we strive for
in spirit and in love.
The doctors reluctantly planned to sacrifice one
so that the other might live to carry the torch for two
but that burden was too great and inevitably they lost both.
Anyone who truly shares a heart
must surely die in the face of such a loss.

Between the lines

ME: experienced *(twice divorced)*, sensitive *(testy)*, uninhibited
(social liability), sporting *(gambler)*, fit *(recovering alcoholic)*,
confident *(egotistical)*, mature outlook *(wears glasses)*, young
at heart *(successful bypass surgery)*, non-conformist *(defrocked
priest)*, love simple things *(cheapskate)*, in touch with feminine
side *(closet cross-dresser)*, would like to touch yours (wants to
borrow your bra).

YOU: Young, mature, beautiful, homely, confident, submissive,
blonde, Asian, university graduate, conservative, transsexual,
must have own car. *(If you think you embody these qualities seek
immediate psychiatric help)*.

Please send a photograph and a stamped self addressed envelope in
case of successful application. No time wasters or emotional cripples!

29

Driven

I grew up in the shipyard where my father worked
within the sound and the smell and the sight
of battalions of rough, toiling, sunscorched men
wielding tools of industrial might.

The forge and the furnaces never shut down
though as night fell the men would all stand
to clock on the night-shift, a rushed cup of tea
then back to the business at hand.

The arc-lights threw black and blue shadows on walls
they were riddled with tracers and spots.
The sparkling of short-lived, man-made fire-flies
preserved in the flashback of thoughts.

My father was one of these legions of men
they lived and they loved and some died.
They dirtied their hands and sweated their brows
as ship after ship caught the tide.

Now my dad is retired but still lives by the sea
that runs through our lives and our veins.
He's earned his respite from those earlier days
and grows roses in warm summer rains.

But an active old engineer never retires
so he spends his time doing good work
ferrying people, less healthy than he
to hospitals, clinics and kirks.

Nearly 80 years old, still unbeaten, unbowed,
he travels for mile upon mile.
Daily he strives to drive away
the cancer that took his fair child.

No regrets

Next week the past pays a visit.
My first love, the earliest romantic repository
of all my youthful hopes, dreams and expectations.
It was love at first sight.
Something which had never happened before, or since.
I still have the faded photographs
of two carefree teenagers hand in hand
before hard reality ruined our reverie.
We're good friends after all these years
but some wounds remain
heavily overgrown with scar tissue
yet alive to the touch.
She's shared a life and lived and lost
but three children and divorce have not dampened her glow.
I can still close my eyes and see
our missed possibilities, lamented but unblemished
amidst those infinite potential scenarios which came to naught.
The sweetness and perfection of what might have been
undiluted and unsullied by what actually was.
I'm glad she married another.
They never talk, they're out of touch
But she'll always touch me,
haunt me.

photograph, Amber Matthews

Ancestral worship

I've got the blood of China in my veins
not through father, mother or distant forebears
but passed on from another's ancient line.
Seven pints passed through the eye of a needle
the anonymous gift of life
for a bastard son, a white ghost!

I feel different
as I look at life
through my wider
less jaundiced eyes

We Chinese treasure our traditions
but whose ancestors should I worship now,
mine, or his?
Maybe I'll just give thanks
pay homage to an eternal Mother
and the universal Father.

Love remains

"Love can never be wrong," you said
Though you were the one
who was wronged in the act
cut to the quick by the facts.
Betrayed, dismayed and all at sea
you found strength enough
to weather that storm
and those to come.
You held the dying hand
that caressed you once
before things changed.
You've loved and lost and lost again
shouldered your grief and others' pain
You've every reason to turn away
but somehow love remains.

Doctored

Alone at 3.00 A.M. in a hospital bed
among thirty other men, equally alone.
Waiting for dawn and the newspaper
time broken down into sub-units
of temperature and blood pressure checks
antibiotics and toilet visits
and the four-hourly pain-killers
to ease you to the next phase.
The purity of pain a constant companion
that never lets you down.

Illness makes strange bedfellows:
A whole ward of tough old boys laid low
and malleable as putty in the hands of diminutive nurses
hopelessly cheerful on the graveyard shift
as they dispense opiates and sympathy.
More feminine than the most exotic Eastern dancer
Beautiful in blue
buxom and slim, comely and homely
each and every one a Goddess
to those of us feeling particularly mortal.

Then finally release and relief at home.
Joyful convalescence amidst familiar things
back in the comfort zone.
But beware complacency.
Heed the wake-up call
open your eyes and embrace life
pamper yourself. Love a little
and treasure a moment or two.
For we pass this way but once.

Another God

Someone died in my sleep last night,
a fellow sufferer in the cancer ward.
All of us who survived the night
looked on in pity
and gratitude
that it was another who was taken.
As he was unhitched from his bottles, tubes and mask,
as he was wheeled away
in an enclosed rectangular trolley
a mobile canvas-covered coffin.
Those of us who could sat up straighter
and tried to look more pink, more healthy
in order to put our own demons off guard,
keep mortality at bay for yet another day.

Abandoned by your health
abandoned by your faith
you need every trick in the book to prevail.
I might try changing beds
or perhaps another God might do.

Someone died in my sleep last night
God bless you if it's you.

Rebirth

Being born once is ample for me
liberation enough for me.
I wonder which previous actions, what karma
provoked this three monthly cycle of death and rebirth
and will I finally emerge a better man?
Twice born. Dvija. Heaven sent.

A CT scanner is like a giant womb
without the warmth, without a heartbeat
except your own
pounding in your ears.
A huge humming ring of lasers and wires
red beams directing and dissecting
discerning white-hot fluid in your veins
embalming, burning like bourbon in your throat.

Born again through a mechanised technological device
every time you wonder
whether you'll be reborn in darkness or in light.
You don't find out for five days
then you get the doctors report.
You pace like an expectant father
hoping to be able to give out cigars
in celebration of your own rebirth.

Passover

Nine candles, bitter herbs
invocations in an ancient tongue:
'BARUH ATAH ADONAI ELOHEINU'
(We praise you O God, sovereign of existence)

A heathen guest sits at table with three generations,
an uncircumcised outsider
adopted and treated as family
head covered and chanting in unison:
'BARUH ATAH ADONAI ELOHEINU'

Named for a Jewish king, a slayer of giants,
I sit with the descendants of that house
singing praise for our deliverance.
Two of us present give thanks
for our own deliverance, from a wilderness
of needles, bedpans and chemotherapy:
'BARUH ATAH ADONAI ELOHEINU'

A privileged surrogate son
warm in the bosom of loving friends.
A covenant now between us
we herald the blossom of spring
the cycle of renewal
and the children.
This year in Hong Kong has been good;
"Next year in Jerusalem."
'BARUH ATAH ADONAI ELOHEINU'

Silver Lining

The support of friends in time of need
is the sweetest silver lining.
A hand on the shoulder, a pat on the back
can lighten any burden
and being humbled to tears by offers of love
from heart-centred souls
not self-centred egos:
those pleasant acquaintances
who crystallise into friends
by caring and reaching and touching.

Life can be good when things look bad.

Enlightenment

I met a Buddha yesterday,
with saffron robes and saffron-coloured fingers.
He was enlightened enough to smoke filtered cigarettes.
"Was I a Buddhist too?" He asked.
"No, I gave up over twenty years ago."
"Well," said he "If you've a good heart
you're Buddhist enough for me."

Birdsong

The cacophonous cadences of old men, hard of hearing
talking too loud in the raucous high pitched dialect of their youth.
Atonal brazen braying and discordant droning
drowns out and drives away the feathered dawn chorus.
They talk of horses, a symbiotic relationship like cattle egrets and cows.
Then the price of gold and assorted village gossip.
Nothing to do anymore but collect rent, read the paper (racing news)
and dream of better times to come, or those long gone.
They sit in courtyards and hail any of their generation
who try to escape off to town.
They keep things in balance, maintain the pecking order,
the whole world's fate in their hands.
When retired Hakka farmers meet they put the world to rights
just like old men everywhere.
The language may be different
but the song remains the same.

Video capture, Gauri Naurain

Culture Club

The Chinese opera came to town
on the back of a fleet of trucks
bouncing and crackling with bamboo and tin sheet.
A temporary cavernous corrugated cathedral
hand-built and rough clad in shimmering layers
of razor thin steel.
The aerialist constructors, shirtless, wiry, fearless
built their theatre in six days.
On the seventh day they rested
and the villagers took over.

Room for two thousand cultured souls sitting
double for standing and shoving and eating
and spitting and hanging from rafters.
Row upon row of identical elderly floral-print ladies
with jangling jade bracelets and bad perms
unaccompanied by the old men busy keeping counsel at the back.
Tobacco-coloured with strong broad faces and squat solid bodies
moulded by years of toil at ropes and nets;
A life of illiterate wisdom, another gift
from the bountiful sea.

The heady humid air, saturated
with eye-watering smells of fried spicy squid, sandalwood,
Tiger balm and other assorted herbal unguents,
wafts languidly in torpid puffs and layers
as if from a priestly censer.

A deafening cacophony of laughter, cackling, cooing
and general din echoes off the roof and rises
to a crescendo as the blood-red curtains part.
The racket continues unabated
reinforced by the crash of cymbals and falling gongs
and the cutting ostinatos of iron-wood blocks.
Strident nasal voices vie with the whole to be heard
above the vociferous accompaniment from the floor
on toy drums, bottles and furniture
and the passing over seat backs of children, food and drink.
The curtains close to no acclaim
just a lengthening of the queues
for toilets food and souvenirs
and popping out to feed the meter
or another can of beer.

Curtains open and curtains close all to no avail.
Then in a pivotal scene of love, death and redemption
the crowd finally falls deathly silent and becomes an audience.
Some look sad and some sing along
with kings and courtesans, heroes and heroines.
Then, spontaneous applause, standing, cheering
and a race for the exits and cars.
Still two scenes left but they've seen what they want.
Only women with kids and those who love song wait till the end
then slowly walk home through the night.

The stars of the show have left the stage
to return to the theatre of life
In the stark white glare of hundred-watt bulbs
the magic has taken flight.
Replaced by carnage and signs of anarchy;
broken chairs, fruit rinds
and prawn heads squashed underfoot.

If you bring culture to the people
they take what they want and leave their debris,
but they came and it's their culture too.

Elocution 101

OK. Let me get this straight, this is like totally awesome. I mean:

SHE SELLS	Oh God! as if!
SEA SHELLS	Oh gross! No way, like gag me with a spoon.
BY	Like, totally 'by'
THE SEA SHORE	Sure!

Then Buddhist

Every now and then I think of then
just like now.
And would I then know Me now?
Every cell in my body has changed so many times
between then and now.
There must be lots of different Me's
wandering around back then.
The younger the Me the further back then
so the older Me now is the younger generation
but, confusingly, I'm older than the oldest of the then generation.
If We strangers could meet what would I
the more experienced younger generation, now
tell Me, the less experienced older generation, then
to make Us a better Me now
based on Our experience then
and would it have made any difference?
What a mind-numbing conundrum.
Maybe every now and then I should think of now.
Just like then!

Heroes

I so admire Steven Hawking
the Lucasian professor of mathematics.
Wheelchair-bound and sustained and constrained by batteries tubes
    and wires.
One of the greatest minds alive
propounding imaginative and profound theories on a sweeping scale.
But a fragile soul, apparently so physically disabled
as to be unable to perform the simplest tasks unaided.
A circumstance that proved not the slightest impediment
to him running off with his nurse.
That takes real imagination.

I so admire Lawrence of Arabia.
Described by Winston Churchill as "the greatest Englishman that
    ever lived".
He led the Arab revolt against the Turks
endured privations, beatings and buggerings
and retired to a life of quiet obscurity
changing his name and shunning the limelight.
Except for his penchant for racing against biplanes
on a motorbike worth more than a house for a working man.
The paramount motorcycle hooligan,
Some obscurity!

I so admire Pablo Piccasso.
A giant of a man with talent so sublime.
He turned the art world on its head, by looking at life
from a different, ever-evolving perspective.
Cubism, his blue period, abstract subjects
with three ears, five legs and a standard pair of lips
on each breast!
But he showed an intimate knowledge of women's anatomy
in his sentimental life
and possessed a nose for a well-turned ankle.

I so admire Richard Feynman
One of the fathers of the atomic bomb
or at least the obstetrician.
A Nobel laureate, a practical theorist
a thinker, a teacher, a perennial student.
But when school was out
he headed South, a bird of a different feather.
Hawaiian-shirted, to Cuba and Rio De Janeiro
at carnival to play drums for a week in the sun.
He understood the rhythms of life.

Bender gender

Homophobia used to be the rage
before I knew all people weren't the same.
Shirt-lifters, carpet-munchers, velcro-surfers
now admired friends and confidantes.
I'm happy to chat to men in pink
rice queens with beautiful golden boys in tow
and kiss cheeks with all the poofs I know.
I stand on street corners with my dykey friends
admiring other women's arses.
When did I become so politically correct?
So reconstructed
that I'm no longer under any illusions
that I could make them jump the fence
after ten minutes with a real man!
Now, I'm the subject of the ten minute speculation
as the coterie of queers gather and ask:
"Who's man enough to do the job?"

No hope

The body of a man lay on its back on the walkover
above the hiss of traffic on the rain swept road below.
The willing victim of a different kind of traffic
a cigarette still in hand, burnt out on the front of his shirt.
Hollow cheeks, sunken eyes still open, white, pupils looking inward.
I wondered how long he'd been dead and who should I call?
But then I noticed the slow rhythmic movement of his chest
laboriously pumping the air into and out of his ravaged body.
I wondered how long he'd been lost?
Only living from hit to hit
seeking regular doses of the oblivion
that was rushing up to meet him
quicker than his own free fall from grace.
At what point does life lose it's meaning?
So that the only way is to view it through
the muddy murky haze of narcotic nihilism.
Where there's life there's hope.
But this is not a life.
Not a hope.

Two Dianas

One vision, two Dianas, Sister Sun, Sister Moon.
Nature spirits
dwelling in a cathedral of trees by empirical churches.
Girlish young faces amidst billowy grey clouds of hair
timeless twin muses
dissimilar all the same.

Where are they from, what brings them here
choice, or necessity
or ministry?
Perpetual daily rounds, heavy laden
Like the fourteen stations of the cross
A liturgical trudge. Te Deum, or simply tedium.

My first tentative connection, a votive offering,
libations of vegetable soup and tea
then as a guest in their parlour
of green laden boughs and green wooden benches
I wax philosophically;
they listen stoically.

Well-spoken, well-bred, unwed, virginal
as well-groomed as exile allows.
No silver spoon now, plastic and paper cups
but dignity and independence intact.
No wild orchids these. No.
Cultivated, but somehow semi-detached.

Cut adrift from society and schedules and rent.
No office, no mortgage, no clubs.
Insular aloof, half hidden, sustained
by immutable bonds of sisterly love.
But nightly alert to strange footfalls
the slapback echo of another life.

Communion

The strident figures of our youth
look much less daunting in their dotage.
Once authoritarian, so stern, strict and severe
Now octogenarians, regressed and degenerated
into warm lovable old men.
Treasured father figures fondly surrogate
for some of us recently orphaned.
Mellowing in our minds
as they collect layer on layer of amber accretions
that help us to see what we need them to be.
A reminder of all that was good in our past.
A reminder of what may yet come to pass.

Re-search

Favoured son of Abraham seeks for God
in places long forgotten, yet unfound.
A 21st century apothecary, the eternal alchemist
dogging dusty footsteps and chasing long shadows
of Nostradamus and magical Merlin.
Reading Maimonides's mysterious 'kabbalah' and his 'Guide to
    wanderers'.
Examining the sacred geometry of pentagrams and twin strands of
    DNA
the building blocks of life, the modern philosopher's stone.
Nature gives up her secrets reluctantly, unwillingly.
Each veneer peeled away reveals
sub-atomic wheels within wheels.
You seek for mutability, the elixir of life
a cure for all that ails mankind.
But I fear we need go deeper
much deeper than the physical realm
to expose the sickness in society that afflicts us all.
So find your cures for cancer, heart disease, the common cold
but beware the seduction of success.
Don't think you can play dice with the world
and let Science be your only God.

Madame Butterfly

You sing so sweetly, melancholy
with a sense of loss so keen
plucking at heartstrings
and choking back tears
you flutter and long to soar away.

But pinned in a frame of your own construction
you see the world in your reflection
not through the glass at what might be.
So pull the pin and step outside
take a chance, you could be free.

The King

Melvis.
Nice contraction that
Me-Elvis.
Except
You-Joking!
Only his body of work remains
to be winnowed, recycled and sold
out of tune, at twenty bucks a throw
by this slim Chinese waiter
living some weird fantasy
in a sequined white jump-suit
fake sideburns glued to his head.
One more pretender to the throne
vending second-hand songs for tips.
Well take one from me.
STOP!
Why not do the monkey king?
you're already half way there.
Instead you choose a foreign mother tongue
and perpetuate the myth of dead white males.
So
Elvis livEs!
At least anagramatically.

Who dares wins

A friend and I are racing motorcycles.
A perilous pursuit for two middle-aged men.
But this race is based on building, not riding them
that comes later.
Hermetic aesthetic symbols of youth and virility
too strong a fetish to resist.
We taunt, tease and cajole
alternately support then oppose.
Evanescent adolescence, a vestigial memory
of toy soldiers and kites and trains.
Victory offers only the pointless prospect
of riding untested, unchallenged, alone.
Who cares wins.
Well I'm in front by a nose.

In trust

I've got God as a guest in my living room.
My girlfriend Gauri's Ganesa and Lakshmi
entrusted to my keeping with strict instructions
on the care and maintenance of Hindu deities.

They've been no trouble at all
these two earthbound Gods
confidantes of the trinity of Brahma, Vishnu and Shiva.
That sounds like The Father, The Son and The Holy Ghost to me.

They've been very courteous and paid their way.
Ganesa, the remover of obstacles and patron of Literature
sitting amongst my books radiating creativity and inspiration
in the direction of my writing desk
and Lakshmi, the Goddess of wealth and prosperity,
I assume she's working on my future prospects!

They've stayed in harmony with my Buddhas
garlanded with beads blessed by a Thai holy man
and my Bodhisattva that inhabits one end of the book shelf
balancing the books on Judaism, Islam, Christianity
and secular philosophy, that occupy the other end.

They've made themselves at home
part of the family.
I'd be sorry to see them go.
Because when they're gone -
she's gone.

Ready made

He wears his father's jacket like a prize
and becomes himself the father and the son.
This coat of many colours many years
he wears it with a reverence and style
draped across his shoulders in embrace
like the arm of someone loved, a confidante
a link between the future and the past.
A relic of a kinder gentler time,
when wisdom was available on call.
He now fulfills that role for his own son
whose turn to take the reins will come in time.
When childhood and its heady days are gone
when he becomes the next link in the chain and
he wears his father's jacket like a prize.

Youth club

My friend's father is slightly younger than me.
I met him just the other day.
A stranger with whom I share a generational link
a common history of world events, music and sports
fashioned from those formative years.
We could have been schoolboys together
under a different plan;
one sock down and dirty knees,
kicking a ball, hide and seek.

But now he can't connect and can't imagine why
as he drinks to excess for executive stress.
So I'll pass on the torch for us both
and bask in the reflected glow.
Does that make me cool and in touch?
or simply gasping
grasping at straws and the very last dregs of summer wine
sipped precariously, enjoyed vicariously
by association with the myriad possibilities of youth.

Youth is wasted on the young
so I'll enjoy just a bit for us all!

Role call

My name's Dave and I'm an alcoholic.
My name's Brenda and I'm anorexic.
My name's Pierre and I'm a wife beater.
My name's Maria and I'm a drug addict.
My name's Harry and I'm a manic depressive.
My name's Agatha and I'm a gambler.
My name's Bruce and I'm a paedophile.
My name's Lucinda and I'm in denial.

My name's Jamal and I'm an Afghani.
My name's Yeshe and I'm a Tibetan.
My name's Bella and I'm a Mozambican.
My name's Ahmed and I'm an Iraqi.
My name's Jose and I'm an East Timorese.
My name's Win Win and I am Burmese.
My name's Nuyen and I'm a Cambodian.
My name's Kim and I'm a North Korean.

Old school ties

I met an old schoolmate yesterday.
Hail fellow, well met.
Only he's not so hale and not so well.
He's been in prison and wasted his life
dreaming at the point of a needle
and planning his next fix.
He lost his health and lost his teeth
helping the police with their inquiries.
He could tell a tale or two if only he could remember.
But now, he tells me, he's kicked the habit
found dignity, found God.
But life weighs him down,
like Sisyphus, perpetually pushing, pushing uphill
never winning just starting over and over.
Nobody wants to know him,
I don't want to know him.
We were never friends,
we'll never be friends.
He needs money, it's only until next week
then he'll pay me back.
I give him the money and give him my number
complicit in my own deception.
Now that he owes me I never have to see him again.
$500 is cheap to walk away from darkness.

No strings

No strings to pull, no ties that bind
just a mature adult business arrangement.
But who's buying and who's selling
this one-night-stand that lasts a year?
Busy people with no time for real intimacy
no time for love.
Just a quick clinical tryst, a fulfillment of physical needs
followed by coffee and civilized conversation.

You never master matters of the heart.
Don't be fooled by invisible ties
they bind the tightest
and constrict imperceptibly, inevitably.
Ask the spider. Ask the fly!
So make it easy, surrender now.
If you're too busy for love
then you're too busy for life.

Photograph, Amber Matthews

Revolution

We freed Nelson Mandela, the Man in the Moon,
saved Kuwait, East Timor and plenty of whales.
Now we're working on Burma, with their own Joan of Arc
and Tibet strikes a chord - The Dalai Lama dilemma.
We taught them fuckin' Serbs a thing or two
by bombing with stealth and good intentions.
Friendly fire to help clean up their act.
We give up whole weekends to march in righteous solidarity
then it's back home through the drizzle
to work on our new signature campaign
'Save the rainforest for Christ's sake'.
Then tea and a chocolate digestive for the nine o'clock news.

Well what about 'that miserable old bastard' two doors down
with his memory set on pause?
He fought a battle or two for freedom in his day.
He lost his innocence and his loved ones
but now all he needs is a comfy chair, a hearty fire and your
        compassion.
And 'those little shits' round the corner
stealing cars, painting walls, running wild.
They're part of your world too.
Broken family kids
confused by domestic violence and chemical comforts.
Look closer to home, open your eyes
The crisis is at your front door.

The P.L.A. (poets' liberation army)

We sit amidst the odours of the East
curry and cardamom, turmeric and masala
enjoying a combination of cultural and culinary treats.
We four foreign disparate souls
diverse in our respective spheres
but poets to a man
declaiming, reading quoting and eating
oblivious to the stares and sniggers
of our unsophisticated fellow diners.
Poets, safe within our own oasis of erudition and cultivation
here in a cultural desert
a barren place, beleaguered by Philistines and rogues.
But the pen is mightier than the sword
and we four brothers-in-arms
unleash our metaphors, unsheathe our razor sharp wits
and let fly our incisive barbs
wielded with a savage eloquence.
Insensitive, unknowing the vanquished eat their fill
and ruminate with bovine stoicism
as we tread lightly once more into the night
and go our separate ways
alone with feet of clay.

Best friends

My best friend's an arsehole.
He's tardy, bigoted, uncaring
self-centred, rude and a drunkard.
But we share a history and an inexorable future
and I love him for the good things he is
or was, or can still be
plus the fact that he's gracious enough to forgive me
when I'm an arsehole too.

photograph, James Lewis

Money laundry

I'm doing a job for a man
with no integrity, no conscience, no soul.
Completely uncultured
whilst surrounded by culture.
He digs up the treasures of the past
and sells them to the highest bidder
bartering his heritage
our heritage! All of us.
To support a profligate lifestyle
Big house, gold chains, twelve cars and a trophy-wife
(3rd place at best I'd say)
His exploits dig deep.
Tomb doors, terracotta horses and temple gods
jimmied out by crowbars, chisels and ropes
and dragged away face down.
He pays me in money he gets from the trade.
Am I, with my thirty pieces of silver, complicit
implicit in this deal?
What if he paid me in statuary
ancient jade or Buddhist icons.
Would I be more culpable or more honest?
at least acknowledging the source of my bounty
or should I take the money and put it to good use?
a sort of karmic cash
or have I already cleansed it of sin
with the honest sweat of my brow?

Ozymandias 2004

I've just been to the land of the free
and seen, by the dawn's early light,
the shadows of history gathering
for another curtain call,
as theoretical freedoms
are debated theatrically
in the house on the hill
by champions of democracy,
sophistry and dentistry.
The superbowl of hyperbole
played deftly
by decades of dickheads
dancing cheek to cheek
with gun-runners and money-lenders
defiling the temple of their fathers.

In another land less free,
preemptive surgical strikes
perform unwanted irrevocable surgery
on the helpless.
'Give them liberty, or give them death'
'How about two for the price of one?'
Good business and nothing personal,
never personal.
'Hi I'm John,
I'll be your terror facilitator for today.'

Meanwhile mom blithely pushes her hypermarket trolley
piled high to excess
with apple pop-tarts,
her fat-free conscience untroubled
by other mothers
with other trolleys
pushing
what's left of their lives
through back-streets,
or huddled masses
massing round braziers
in the shadow of Liberty's beacon
and under six-lane flyovers
and in abandoned buildings,
with valiant veterans of another unjust war.

A pleasure

M'*sai* M'*goi*   M'*sai*

There is a beautiful American guy
the brightest comet
passing through our midst.
Barefoot, like a carefree child
on a beach, scattering stardust like sand,
his tongue firmly in our cheek.

M'*sai* M'*goi*   M'*sai*

There is a beautiful American guy
a true Adonis, torn between Persephone and Aphrodite
darkness and light, noble and degraded love.
Inspired by Caliope
he amuses us, eloquently
with wicked tales of 'elastic gender',
satyrs and marbled perfection;
pederasty on a pedestal!

M'sai M'goi   *M'sai*

There is a beautiful American guy
fresh youth at the outset of life
touched by greatness.
A talent too prodigious to envy
we just dip our fingers and savour the smell.
Then he's gone,
leaving his faint aroma and
footprints in the sand.

M'sai M'goi   *M'sai M'goi*

Doh je   *Joi gin*

*Dedicated to Ted Mathys and inspired by his 'Hong Kong Nocturne' in the
OUTLOUD poetry anthology 2002*

Judgement days

Sometimes I feel angels gazing over my shoulder
and into my soul in loving judgment
but it is judgment none the less
and gives pause for thought.
I only seem to feel the bright white heat on my back
when I'm misbehaving
then they gather in flocks
cherubs with notebooks and scales.
How many infringements have I logged today
and what do I score for an act of kindness?
Where are they when I'm being charitable, kind and sharing?
Maybe they're gazing over your shoulder.

Eulogy

I attended the funeral of a lady I'd never met
the wife of a man with whom I shared more history than intimacy.
I voiced prayers and sang and took part in arcane rituals
as a gesture of support and respect.
The eulogy was my introduction and goodbye rolled into one
and to the uninitiated sounded at times like a curriculum vitae.
It was read by an elderly man, gentle and frail but strong in spirit
who concluded the reading and asked our indulgence as he sang a
     prayer
a liturgical lament in Latin.
Sweet-voiced and redolent with meaning and emotion
he sang and lifted the moment and our spirits to a new level
with the conquering presence of love
and faith in something bigger.

Working class God

Across the nautical miles
on an island of fishermen
by the sheltered narrows of the China Sea
sits a house of God
built by the father's father's of today's tillers of the waves.
This temple is listed by the antiquities and monuments office
as a cultural icon of benefit to tourism
and scheduled for cleaning, re-tiling and restoration.
But it's listed as a part of life by these simple, honest folk
and scheduled for re-dedication and blessing.
For this is no Medici palace for an elegant, effete and cultured deity
this is the home of a working-class God with work to be done.
Controlling the elements, protecting the nets
and holding all vessels in a warm embrace.
Government bureaucrats, feathering their caps
want to preserve for posterity
the muted patinated tints and quaint dingy dank corners.
The villagers want a new brush to sweep clean
and paint in bright, lively, vibrant hues
of gaudily gold, red and green.
This house is not for a redundant God of antiquity.
This God requires daily sustenance, libations and offerings.
He is part of the clan and everywhere visible
In the sparkling of infinite pin pricks of light
as a gentle rain dapples the calm green sea.
Deep amongst the ancient banyans
those sentinels with twisted limbs entwined in a sensual embrace,
gnarled boughs that mirror the stooped backs of ancient mariners
themselves as hard and weathered as aged teak.

Now foreigners have come to Kau Sai Chau
Italians, offering their skills with open hands
that carry the genetic legacy
of Leonardo, Michelangelo, Botticelli, Caravaggio.
They delve with care amidst the treasures
and peel away the secrets of the years.
Uncovered scripts and ancient colours
reveal the hand of venerated generations.
Those long gone but ever present in nooks and crannies
in ancestral tablets and in the faces of boys at play.
The job is done, outsiders gone.
Life returns to the slow rhythmic pulse of the sea
and God rests his feet in front of the fire
at home with a cup of tea.

Flagging

Some still fly the flag in good old Hong Kong
Some still think it's 1945
and the sun never sets and we won the war
and civilized the natives before tea.
"So lucky we're here to show them the way
things ought to be done in the East.
To stand on ceremony, on their own two feet.
God knows what they stood on before!"
Then it's back to the club, pink gins all around
another hard day in the sun
manning the floodgates, holding the fort,
a life in defence of the realm.

A funny old man out of step, out of time
punching the clock, counting the days.
Lamenting lost values, lost loves and lost youth,
retiring in just one more year.
Planning a life of comfort and ease
in that green and pleasant land - Sri Lanka!
Pleasantly pejorative, vaguely vituperative.
A rusty cog in a system gone digital.
Your Hong Kong is gone, the thin red line
the battle of Britain is lost.
So bravely retreat, you're not needed now,
leave the lights on there are people still here.

Butterflies and Dreams

That fresh first taste, undaunted love
grand plans and schemes and dreams.
The journey's end has just begun
as wings and hopes take flight.

Fleeting glimpse, ephemeral sheen
Icarus-like up to the sun.
Then spiraling flameout, essence of tears
burnt fingers and stark flaming heart.

Water littered with lifeless forms,
broken-backed and flightless now
clumped like multi-coloured fabrics
swirling through eddies mid-stream.

Turning, kaleidoscopic, tumbling
over unfeeling blind cataracts
inexorably down to the sea.
Butterflies and dreams, gone home to die.

Gifted

My father sang *La Bohème* and built ships
my mother danced on the stage then had kids.
Both of them sacrificed what might have been
for the sake of their family life.
They passed on the gifts of music, art
humour and competent hands.
We share the same genes
although we speak a subtle different tongue
of generations and geography and time.
Both still drawn to the sound of the sea
that lies between us.
Sometimes I think I'd like to be
I ought to be
a Bohemian on their behalf.
They just want me to be happy.
So this year, like in the Janis Joplin song
I bought them a Mercedes Benz
which made me very happy.

Acknowledgements

To many of the people mentioned here, and in some cases lovingly woven throughout the poems themselves, I owe a debt of gratitude far beyond the inspiration, support and encouragement which allowed me to finish this book. To some I quite literally owe my life.

My eternal thanks and much love goes out to Michael and Betty Kadoorie and their children Natalie, Bettina and Philip. My brother Bob and his wife Deepa. Claudio DeBedin (my oldest and dearest friend) his wife Claire, son Gaetano and his Mum June (who meant so much to us). Maria (the Italian) Barbieri. Mark and Jal Godfrey, their daughter Emma and son Roy (my Godson). Hamish and Paula Ewart. Deborah and Jason Whittle. Dr Benny and Jenifer Tong. Peter Cotton. Keiron and Karen Combes. Christopher Lavender. Professor Philip Johnson. Dr. Anthony Chan. Dr. Tony Mok. The staff of the oncology department and wards of The Prince of Wales Hospital. Philip O'Mullan (my musical partner in crime and spiritual younger brother). David Yip. Bertha Tamayo. Cat (leng lui), Benny, Maria, Siu Wan, Ah Fai, Owen and everybody else at The Fringe Club. Bakr Rabie. Paul Balaam (still teaching me after 40 years). Ray, Mila, Soli, Salome and Manuel. Susie Wilkins (rock chick with attitude). Pauline Burton (rock mum with attitude). Patrick Murdoch (guitar gunslinger par excellence). William Tang (play them blues white boy). Jo Dehayney (you got the power). Dave Colquoun (the Dorian Gray of the HK music scene). John (too many strings) French. Peter and Cindy Scher. Rosemary Sayer and Terry Grosse. Peter Gordon and Elaine Leung. Amber and Sarah (you big tarts). Elaine Liu and Ivan Foti. Fat Hamish at Hongkongbikes.com (gut instinct!). Lynne Austin. Louise Ho. Emma Ayres ("That's Mr. Frankie Cairo to you buddy!"). Peter and Natica Pappas. Xu Xi. Mike Ingham. David Osborne (haven't you finished that bike yet?). Mani Rao. Sayed, Farook and Salah (P.L.A. founder members). Shirley Lim. Page Richards. Vivian Lam. All of my fellow OUTLOUD poets. My fellow committee members of The Hong Kong International Literary Festival. And last but certainly not least my partner and muse Gauri Narain.

Note from the publisher

Accidental Occidental was first published for primarily Hong Kong distribution in hardcover in 2005 with the assistance of a grant from The Hong Kong Arts Development Council. This volume, now out of print, is being re-issued in an international paperback edition.

David McKirdy's commitment to both his own work and that of his fellow Hong Kong poets led a few years ago to the introduction of Chameleon's Hong Kong poetry publishing project, under his editorial guidance.

Other volumes in the *Chameleon Press Hong Kong poetry series* include:

The Mental Life of Cities by Eddie Tay (2010)
Ghostmasters by Mani Rao (2010)
Snowblind from my protective colouring by Andrew Barker (2009)
Miss Moon's Class by Viki Holmes (2008)
Summer Cicadas by Jennifer Wong (2006)
100 Poems: 1985-2005 by Mani Rao (2006)
Accidental Occidental by David McKirdy (2005)
Poetry Live: An Anthology of Hong Kong Poetry for Teens (2005)
Clearing Ground by Martin Alexander (2004)
Raincheck Renewed by Kavita Jindal (2004)
Food Court by Timothy Kaiser (2003)